Green GROWTH

Green GROWTH

Matthew Petchinsky

Green Growth: Marketing Strategies for Your Hemp Business and Dispensary
By Matthew Petchinsky

Introduction – Sowing the Seeds of Hemp Marketing Success

The world of hemp is no longer confined to the margins. Once relegated to misunderstanding, stigma, and restrictive policy, hemp has reemerged in the 21st century as a symbol of innovation, sustainability, and wellness. From biodegradable construction materials and eco-friendly textiles to powerful CBD formulations for therapeutic relief, hemp is driving an economic and cultural renaissance. As legalization expands and consumer interest swells, the hemp industry is no longer a niche—it's a movement.

But with that growth comes complexity. While the public is increasingly embracing hemp, the market itself is flooded with products, misinformation, and regulatory ambiguity. It is within this evolving and often unpredictable landscape that entrepreneurs, dispensary owners, and product developers are called to act—not just as merchants, but as educators, brand builders, and cultural ambassadors.

This book, *Green Growth: Marketing Strategies for Your Hemp Business and Dispensary*, is your practical and strategic guide to thriving in that space.

Whether you're launching your very first CBD brand or looking to scale an established dispensary, you will find within these pages a roadmap for navigating the unique challenges of hemp advertising, branding, and outreach. You will discover how to define your identity, connect authentically with consumers, and outmaneuver digital and legal restrictions that continue to hinder many in the space.

In today's saturated landscape, it's no longer enough to simply have a quality product—you must know how to communicate its value, how to legally and ethically reach your market, and how to stand out with credibility, clarity, and confidence. You must master both the art and science of hemp marketing.

This book covers:

- **Brand Development** – How to define and express a brand that resonates with your audience while staying true to your vision and values.
- **Advertising Compliance** – How to interpret and work within legal frameworks that vary by jurisdiction, platform, and product type.
- **Digital Marketing Mastery** – How to build visibility online through SEO, website strategy, content creation, social media, and email marketing.
- **Traditional and Grassroots Promotion** – How to effectively blend print, radio, and community events into your outreach strategy.
- **Data and Analytics** – How to use data, feedback, and analytics to fine-tune campaigns and drive growth.
- **Community Building** – How to engage with consumers on a deeper level, cultivating loyalty and turning customers into advocates.

This is more than a book on hemp marketing. It's a call to innovate, educate, and adapt. The hemp industry is a frontier full of promise—but only for those who can navigate the terrain. If you're ready to grow your brand from seed to shelf to soul, then you're exactly where you need to be.

Let's begin your green growth journey.

Chapter 1: Branding from the Ground Up

Cultivating a Brand that Roots Deep and Reaches Far

In the ever-growing hemp industry, your brand is more than just a logo or a product—it's your identity, your message, and your promise to the customer. In a space that is still battling outdated perceptions, media restrictions, and misinformation, branding becomes not just a marketing tool, but a vehicle for education, trust, and transformation.

Establishing a strong, authentic, and memorable brand from the very beginning is critical for your long-term success. Hemp businesses are not only selling wellness or sustainability—they are selling trust, clarity, and value in a market that demands transparency. In this chapter, we will explore how to build your brand from the ground up, with practical steps to help you define your identity, voice, mission, and competitive edge.

The Importance of a Clear and Compelling Brand Identity

In a field crowded with tinctures, topicals, vapes, teas, edibles, textiles, and construction-grade bioplastics, consumers need a reason to choose *you*. A strong brand identity isn't just about aesthetics; it's about recognition, differentiation, and emotional resonance.

A clear brand identity:

- Establishes consistency across all customer touchpoints (website, packaging, social media, events).
- Communicates your values and intentions without saying a word.
- Helps consumers identify with your story and mission.
- Builds long-term loyalty by making your product feel familiar and trusted.

Think of your brand as a living presence—it should evoke a consistent feeling in every customer interaction. Whether someone sees your packaging at a local co-op or visits your Instagram feed, they should immediately sense who you are, what you offer, and why it matters.

Crafting Your Visual Elements and Brand Voice

Visual Elements:
Your visual presentation is the first impression of your brand—often formed in seconds. These include your logo, color palette, font choices, icons, packaging design, and even your photography style.

In the hemp space, visuals can evoke anything from holistic wellness and nature-inspired minimalism to futuristic biotech or vintage apothecary aesthetics. Your visuals should match your product promise and audience expectations. For example:

- Organic CBD oils may benefit from earthy tones, clean lines, and calming imagery.
- Hemp sportswear may emphasize modern, bold graphics and performance-driven energy.
- A luxury skincare line might use muted palettes, gold accents, and elegant fonts.

Brand Voice:

Your voice is how your brand speaks across all platforms—from website copy to social captions to email marketing. It should be as distinct and consistent as your logo.

Decide early: Are you conversational or clinical? Playful or polished? Educational or edgy?

For example:

- A brand targeting millennials might use casual language with humor and memes.
- A wellness-focused audience might prefer a soft, nurturing tone grounded in facts.
- B2B hemp suppliers might choose a more technical, professional approach.

Once you define your brand voice, document it. Create brand guidelines that you and your team follow religiously. Consistency builds familiarity. Familiarity builds trust.

Defining Your Mission, Values, and Tone

Your **mission** is the heartbeat of your business—the reason you exist beyond profits.

Ask yourself:

- What problem are you solving?
- What change do you want to see in the world?
- How does hemp serve that change?

Examples:

- "We believe in natural healing for modern lives."
- "We are restoring sustainability through hemp-based innovation."
- "We provide plant-based relief for chronic stress and anxiety."

Your **values** define your ethics, priorities, and the standards you uphold. These could include:

- Transparency in sourcing and labeling
- Sustainable packaging and cultivation
- Advocacy for hemp policy reform
- Community outreach and education

And your **tone** is how those values sound when spoken aloud. If your values are serious, but your tone is sarcastic or overly casual, there's a mismatch that will confuse your audience.

Mission + values + tone = your brand's personality. That personality should be as clear to customers as it is to your team.

Creating a Unique Selling Proposition (USP)

In an industry overflowing with similar products, your USP (Unique Selling Proposition) is what makes you different—and better—for a specific audience.

A strong USP answers:

- What do we do?
- For whom do we do it?
- Why are we the best at it?

Weak USP: "We sell premium CBD oil."
Strong USP: "We deliver USDA-certified organic CBD drops formulated by herbalists and backed by lab testing, designed for women managing chronic anxiety without prescription drugs."
To develop your USP:

1. Study competitors. What are they saying, and what are they *not* saying?
2. Talk to your customers. What do they love about your brand? What do they want that's missing?
3. Find your "only" statement. What can you say about your product that no one else can say truthfully?

Your USP should live on your homepage, your product packaging, and in your pitch to every new customer. It's the cornerstone of your differentiation strategy.

Building Brand Trust in a Sensitive and Competitive Space

The hemp industry still carries a burden of mistrust. Due to decades of prohibition, bad actors, and inconsistent regulation, many consumers approach hemp with caution.

Your job is to build *trust*.

Here's how:

- **Transparency:** Publish lab results, share sourcing info, and show your face. Be human.
- **Consistency:** Make sure your product quality, messaging, and customer experience are uniform.
- **Education:** Help your customers understand the science, benefits, and legality of hemp.
- **Authenticity:** Don't overpromise or use fear-based marketing. Be honest about what your products can and cannot do.
- **Community:** Respond to comments, offer support, and celebrate your customers. Loyalty is built through engagement.

Brand trust doesn't happen overnight—it grows over time through repetition, integrity, and care.

Final Thoughts

Branding isn't a one-time task—it's a long-term relationship between your business and your audience. The deeper your roots go into mission, identity, and values, the stronger your brand will grow in the unpredictable winds of market shifts, legal changes, and consumer behavior.

In the hemp industry, a strong brand isn't optional—it's your foundation.

So ask yourself:

- What feeling does your brand give people?
- What do you stand for?
- What makes you unforgettable?

Answer those questions honestly, and you'll not only stand out—you'll stand strong.

Chapter 2: Understanding Hemp Advertising Laws

Cultivating Compliance in a Complicated Landscape

The hemp industry offers enormous promise—but it also comes with a legal minefield that every entrepreneur must learn to navigate. Marketing hemp is not like marketing shoes, vitamins, or coffee. It's a high-stakes balancing act between innovation and regulation, requiring a clear understanding of the laws that govern what you can say, where you can say it, and how to say it without triggering penalties, takedowns, or worse.

This chapter provides a comprehensive look at the regulatory framework surrounding hemp advertising, helping you remain legally compliant while still building a strong, visible, and trusted brand.

Overview of Federal, State, and Local Regulations

The legality of hemp advertising is not governed by one universal law—it's a layered framework, much like the hemp plant itself: fibrous, complex, and deeply rooted in historical policy.

Federal Regulations

At the federal level, hemp was officially legalized in the U.S. under the **Agriculture Improvement Act of 2018**, better known as the **2018 Farm Bill** (we'll explore this in depth shortly). However, legalization does not equal unrestricted marketing. The **Food and Drug Administration (FDA)** still prohibits companies from making unverified health claims about hemp-derived products, especially cannabidiol (CBD).

For example, marketing your CBD oil as a "cure for anxiety" or a "treatment for chronic pain" could lead to warnings or fines. Instead, you must use careful language like "may support relaxation" or "promotes general wellness."

State Regulations

Each state in the U.S. has the power to regulate hemp advertising within its borders. This creates a fragmented legal landscape. What's permitted in Oregon may be restricted in Texas. Some states allow in-store promotions and billboard ads; others ban hemp advertising near schools or in public parks.

Some key variables by state:

- Whether CBD can be added to food or beverages
- Required disclaimers on packaging or ads
- Restrictions on health-related claims
- Labeling and QR code requirements
- Limits on advertising to minors or general audiences

Local Regulations

Municipalities can impose their own restrictions, particularly around outdoor signage, local broadcast advertising, and community events. For example, your city may allow a dispensary to operate legally—but prohibit promotional banners, flags, or sponsorship of local parades.

To stay safe:

- Always verify local advertising codes with your city or county business office
- Consult legal counsel or compliance experts before launching ad campaigns

Key Provisions from the 2018 Farm Bill

The 2018 Farm Bill was a pivotal moment in American agricultural and commercial history. It declassified hemp as a Schedule I substance under the Controlled Substances Act, paving the way for a new era of cultivation, commerce, and branding.

The core provisions relevant to advertising include:

1. **Legal Definition of Hemp**:
   Hemp is defined as *Cannabis sativa L.* with a THC concentration of **no more than 0.3% on a dry weight basis**. Anything above that threshold is legally considered marijuana and remains federally illegal.

2. **Interstate Commerce is Protected**:
   The bill prohibits states from interfering with the transportation of legally produced hemp across state lines. This also protects many online hemp businesses that ship products nationwide—but again, advertising must remain compliant with both origin and destination state rules.

3. **Oversight by the USDA and States**:
   States are required to submit hemp production plans to the **U.S. Department of Agriculture (USDA)** for approval. These plans also cover enforcement, testing, and compliance rules—which indirectly affect labeling and marketing language.

4. **FDA Authority Remains**:
   The FDA retains jurisdiction over how hemp-derived products are marketed, especially those that are ingested. Companies must not position hemp or CBD as dietary supplements or use disease-related claims without scientific substantiation and FDA approval.

What this means in practice: **Even if your product is legal, your** *language* **must be lawful, honest, and evidence-based.**

Differences Between Legal Cannabis and Hemp Marketing

While both cannabis and hemp come from the same plant species (*Cannabis sativa*), they are regulated very differently—especially when it comes to advertising.

Cannabis (Marijuana) Marketing

- Heavily regulated at the state level (because cannabis is still illegal federally)
- Must avoid content that appeals to minors (e.g., no cartoon mascots, child-friendly packaging)
- May be restricted from using traditional ad channels (TV, radio, billboard)
- Often limited to in-state marketing only
- Subject to strict restrictions on discounts, giveaways, and promotions

Hemp Marketing

- Legal federally under the 2018 Farm Bill
- Can be sold and shipped across state lines (subject to state-specific restrictions)
- Cannot make unverified medical claims (especially with CBD)
- May advertise on digital platforms (with limitations)
- Faces fewer location-based advertising bans—but must still comply with FDA and FTC rules

Bottom line: While cannabis advertising is confined to state-level bubbles, hemp marketing has broader potential—but with stricter oversight on language and health claims.

Ad Restrictions on Major Platforms

Despite hemp's legal status, many digital platforms still treat it as a high-risk or restricted product. This creates frustration for brands trying to reach customers online.

Facebook / Instagram (Meta)

- Prohibits direct promotion of CBD or ingestible hemp products
- May allow promotion of topical hemp products with a verified business account
- Avoid keywords like "CBD," "cannabis," "cure," "THC," "pain relief," etc.
- Creative workaround: Use educational posts or promote blogs rather than direct product links

Google Ads

- Generally prohibits the promotion of CBD products, even topical
- Ads for non-ingestible hemp products (hemp clothing, hemp seed oil) may be allowed
- Avoid misleading claims or unapproved health terminology
- Consider using Google Ads for *general wellness branding*—not product sales

YouTube

- Educational content is allowed
- Direct product promotion in video or description may lead to demonetization
- Use subtle branding and mention only non-ingestible products
- Link to a compliant landing page, not a direct store listing

TikTok

- Zero-tolerance policy on cannabis and CBD promotion
- Even organic (non-paid) content may be removed or shadow-banned
- Focus on lifestyle, farming, sustainability, or behind-the-scenes content without naming specific products

Alternative Platforms

- Podcasts, email marketing, and SEO blogs remain some of the most effective and safe long-term tools
- Platforms like DuckDuckGo, Rumble, or cannabis-friendly social networks offer additional avenues

Staying Compliant While Remaining Creative

Creativity and compliance can—and must—coexist. Your challenge is to share your message, build trust, and generate awareness *without triggering legal flags*.

Tips for Staying Compliant:

1. **Use Benefit-Oriented, Not Medical, Language**
   - Instead of: "Treats chronic pain"
   - Say: "Supports joint mobility and relaxation"
2. **Highlight Transparency**
   - Showcase third-party lab results
   - Offer detailed sourcing info without exaggerated claims
3. **Use Storytelling**
   - Share your brand's journey, values, and community involvement
   - Let customer testimonials speak for your products (but avoid posting unverifiable health claims)
4. **Educate First, Sell Second**
   - Position your content as informative rather than sales-driven
   - Use blogs, podcasts, and videos to teach—not pitch
5. **Build a Newsletter List**
   - Email is one of the few platforms that gives you complete control over your messaging
   - Segment your audience and personalize content without violating ad policies
6. **Review Policies Frequently**
   - Platform guidelines and state laws change regularly
   - Schedule quarterly reviews of your content, ads, and compliance practices

Final Thoughts

Advertising in the hemp industry is not a free-for-all. It's a carefully regulated environment where words matter, images matter, and context matters. But within these constraints lies incredible opportunity. The brands that succeed are not those that push boundaries recklessly—but those that educate, innovate, and inspire while respecting the rules.

As the legal landscape continues to evolve, staying informed and adaptable will be your greatest asset. Compliance is not a limitation—it's a competitive advantage. When you prove yourself trustworthy and transparent, you build something more valuable than a customer base—you build a legacy.

Chapter 3: Website Optimization and SEO Fundamentals

Planting Your Digital Roots for Visibility and Growth

In the digital economy, your website is your storefront, your voice, and—most importantly—your trust anchor. For hemp entrepreneurs, having a well-optimized website is not a luxury; it's a necessity. Amid heavy advertising restrictions and platform bans, your website becomes one of the few marketing tools you fully control. It must be fast, secure, informative, and discoverable by search engines—all while complying with complex hemp and CBD regulations.

In this chapter, we'll walk through the essential strategies to turn your website into a high-performing hub for growth, visibility, and customer engagement. From SEO fundamentals to accessibility compliance, from writing persuasive content to mastering technical optimization, you'll learn how to turn your digital presence into your most reliable marketing tool.

Designing a High-Performing, Accessible Website

A hemp business website must do more than just look good—it needs to function smoothly, load quickly, and work well for *every* visitor. A high-performing site builds trust, drives conversions, and increases your authority in the space.

Key Design Priorities:

1. **Mobile-First Design**
   - Most users will access your site via mobile. Ensure your layout, navigation, and buttons are thumb-friendly, responsive, and intuitive on all screen sizes.

2. **Fast Load Speed**
   - Pages that take more than 3 seconds to load lose over 50% of users.
   - Compress images, use caching, reduce scripts, and optimize your hosting for performance.

3. **Clear Navigation**
   - Your homepage, shop, about page, and contact info should be easy to find.
   - Use clean menus, call-to-action buttons, and breadcrumb navigation for easy browsing.

4. **Accessibility (ADA & WCAG Compliance)**
   - Include alt-text on all images for screen readers.
   - Ensure text is legible with proper contrast ratios.
   - Make the site navigable by keyboard for users with mobility limitations.

5. **Trust Elements**
   - Display lab results, third-party certifications, and return/refund policies.
   - Include clear disclaimers for legal and compliance transparency.
   - Feature testimonials and real customer reviews to build credibility.

Your website is not just a digital brochure—it's your living, breathing brand headquarters. Every click, scroll, and second spent on your site influences how your audience perceives your trustworthiness and professionalism.

On-Page and Off-Page SEO Techniques

Search Engine Optimization (SEO) is the practice of improving your website's visibility on search engines like Google. In the hemp industry—where paid advertising options are limited—*organic traffic through SEO is one of the most powerful tools you have.*

On-Page SEO focuses on elements *within* your website.

Key Techniques:

- **Keyword Research:** Use tools like SEMrush, Ahrefs, or Ubersuggest to identify high-value, low-competition keywords relevant to your products and audience.
- **Title Tags:** Every page should have a unique, keyword-rich title (70 characters max).
- **Meta Descriptions:** Write engaging summaries under 160 characters that encourage clicks.
- **Header Tags (H1, H2, H3):** Use headers to structure your content for readability and searchability.
- **Image Optimization:** Compress images, add descriptive filenames, and use keyword-rich alt text.
- **Internal Linking:** Link between your blog posts, product pages, and informational content to keep users on your site longer and help search engines crawl it more effectively.

Off-Page SEO builds your site's reputation and authority *outside* your domain.

Key Techniques:

- **Backlinks:** Secure high-quality inbound links from authoritative websites in the wellness, sustainability, and cannabis education spaces.
- **Guest Blogging:** Write informative articles for trusted platforms and link back to your site.
- **Social Sharing:** Promote your content organically on platforms—even if ads are restricted—to encourage traffic and shares.
- **Local SEO:** Register your business with Google My Business, include location keywords, and encourage customer reviews to help local customers find you.

Writing Content That Ranks and Converts

SEO brings traffic. Great content keeps it—and converts it into action.

Content That Ranks

- **Match Search Intent:** Know what your visitors are looking for—information, product comparisons, FAQs—and provide it clearly.
- **Be Comprehensive:** Longer content (1,000+ words) tends to rank better, but make sure it's valuable and easy to navigate.
- **Use Natural Language:** Write like a human, not a machine. Google now uses AI-based algorithms that reward well-structured, helpful content.
- **Focus on Topics, Not Just Keywords:** Write around themes like "hemp for stress relief" or "eco-friendly uses of hemp," not just isolated keywords.

Content That Converts

- **Use Benefit-Focused Headlines:** Instead of "Hemp Oil 1000mg," try "Calm Your Mind and Sleep Better with 1000mg Hemp Oil."
- **Place CTAs Strategically:** Use calls-to-action like "Shop Now," "Download Guide," or "Get a Free Sample" after sections of valuable content.
- **Include Trust Indicators:** Testimonials, badges, lab test links, and verified payment methods increase confidence.
- **Avoid Health Claims:** Instead of saying your product "treats pain," say it "supports natural recovery" or "promotes wellness."

Great content balances education and sales without ever crossing into the territory of illegal health claims.

Technical SEO for Hemp Businesses

Technical SEO ensures that search engines can easily find, index, and understand your content. It's the behind-the-scenes foundation that supports your on-page efforts.

Essential Technical Areas:

1. **XML Sitemaps**
   - Submit a sitemap to Google Search Console to help search engines crawl your site efficiently.
2. **Robots.txt**
   - Use this file to guide what pages you want search engines to crawl (or not crawl).
3. **Secure URLs (HTTPS)**
   - Google prioritizes secure websites. Make sure your site has a valid SSL certificate.
4. **URL Structure**
   - Use clean, readable URLs with keywords (e.g., your-brand.com/hemp-oil-benefits).
5. **Schema Markup**
   - Add structured data (JSON-LD) to your product pages to improve how listings appear in search engines (e.g., price, reviews, availability).
6. **404 and Redirects**
   - Set up proper redirects for deleted pages and monitor broken links to avoid frustrating users and harming SEO.
7. **Core Web Vitals**
   - Google scores your website on load speed, interactivity, and visual stability. Optimize these for better rankings and user experience.

Investing in technical SEO gives your site the solid infrastructure needed to rank, scale, and grow.

Creating Authority Through Educational Content

Hemp brands face more advertising roadblocks than traditional businesses. But one area remains wide open and underutilized: **education.** When you position yourself as a helpful, knowledgeable authority, you build lasting relationships, earn backlinks, and boost SEO.

Types of Educational Content That Builds Authority:

- **How-to Guides:** "How to Use Hemp Oil for Daily Wellness"
- **Explainers:** "What Is the Difference Between Hemp and Marijuana?"
- **Infographics:** Visual explainers of the endocannabinoid system or hemp growth cycles
- **FAQs:** Dedicated pages answering common customer questions about legality, effects, and usage
- **Video Content:** Tutorials, behind-the-scenes farming processes, or customer testimonials

Bonus: Educational content often ranks higher because it satisfies **informational search intent**, which dominates Google searches in the wellness and hemp space.

By becoming a trusted source of information, you not only attract organic traffic—you also reduce your reliance on paid ads, strengthen consumer trust, and build a brand that people recommend.

Final Thoughts

Your website is more than just a digital space—it's your strongest marketing asset in an industry with limited advertising options and intense competition. Optimizing your site for both users and search engines puts your hemp brand on the map—literally and figuratively.

From mobile optimization and ADA compliance to rich educational content and smart keyword use, every choice you make on your website either brings your audience closer or drives them away.

Plant the right digital seeds now, and your business will harvest the rewards in organic traffic, loyal customers, and long-term authority.

Chapter 4: Digital Advertising in a Restricted Space

Marketing Hemp in a World That Doesn't Always Want You to

Marketing hemp in today's digital environment is like navigating a maze with shifting walls. Although the 2018 Farm Bill legalized hemp federally, major digital platforms still enforce vague and often inconsistent rules around advertising. Facebook, Instagram, Google Ads, and TikTok remain cautious due to the industry's complex relationship with cannabis and evolving state and federal regulations. As a result, hemp businesses often find their ads rejected, accounts shadowbanned, or content suppressed.

But this challenge is also an opportunity. It forces innovation, encourages authenticity, and pushes hemp entrepreneurs to think differently about brand visibility, trust-building, and long-term strategy.

This chapter will guide you through the safest, smartest, and most effective digital advertising tactics available to hemp businesses today—focusing on what works, what to avoid, and how to carve your own lane through a heavily policed terrain.

Workarounds for Google, Facebook, Instagram, and TikTok

Google Ads (Search & Display)

Google maintains strict policies regarding the advertisement of CBD or hemp products—particularly ingestibles. Ads for hemp-derived topicals may be accepted under specific conditions, but even then, accounts can be flagged.

Workarounds and Best Practices:

- Avoid using terms like "CBD," "cannabis," or "hemp oil" in headlines or copy.
- Focus ads on *benefits*, not ingredients. For example, "Support stress relief" instead of "Buy CBD drops."
- Promote educational content, not products. Drive traffic to blog posts or free guides with soft CTAs like "Learn More."
- Use landing pages that are compliance-optimized (no unverifiable health claims).
- Run *brand awareness* campaigns rather than *conversion* campaigns.

Facebook & Instagram (Meta Platforms)

Meta's advertising policy prohibits the promotion of CBD and ingestible hemp products, even if legal. However, non-ingestible items like hemp clothing or skincare can be promoted with proper documentation.

Tips to Navigate Meta Restrictions:

- Promote lifestyle content and customer stories without mentioning the product directly.
- Run engagement ads that promote blogs, brand videos, or downloadable resources.
- Use approved business categories (e.g., "Health & Wellness" or "Alternative Medicine").
- Consider "whitelisting" influencers to share your brand organically.
- Build lookalike audiences based on people who interact with your organic content.

TikTok

TikTok is the most restrictive platform. Any mention of CBD, hemp, or cannabis-related products is grounds for removal or account suspension.

Workarounds:

- Focus on *visual storytelling*. Show your farm, production process, or packaging without naming the product.
- Use coded language or trending audio to build engagement without direct product promotion.
- Share educational or sustainability-focused content (e.g., hemp as an eco-material).
- Leverage "link-in-bio" tools like Linktree to redirect viewers to compliant landing pages or newsletters.

Best Practices for Email Marketing and Newsletters

Unlike most advertising platforms, **email marketing gives you complete control** over your messaging, audience, and distribution. It's your most powerful—and most underutilized—tool in a restricted space.

Building Your Email List

- Offer value in exchange for email addresses: free guides, discounts, recipes, eBooks, etc.
- Use exit-intent popups, embedded forms, and newsletter opt-ins throughout your site.
- Never buy or rent email lists—it damages your deliverability and trust.

Crafting Effective Campaigns

- Use *clear, engaging subject lines* that speak to curiosity or emotion, not just products.
- Share *education first, offers second*: e.g., "Why Hemp May Help with Stress" followed by a CTA to your product line.
- Segment your list based on behavior and interest (e.g., new subscribers vs. repeat customers).
- A/B test subject lines, images, and CTAs for optimal performance.
- Always include clear unsubscribe options and your business address (CAN-SPAM compliance).

Email marketing is your digital newsletter, your private channel, and your best friend. It's where the most intimate, direct conversations with customers happen.

Organic Traffic Through Blogging and Influencer Outreach
When ads are restricted, *content becomes currency*. An effective content marketing strategy builds long-term traffic, trust, and visibility—without ad spend.

Blogging for Organic Search

- Answer common questions: "What does hemp oil do?" "Is hemp legal in my state?" "What are the environmental benefits of hemp?"
- Focus on low-competition keywords using tools like Ubersuggest or Ahrefs.
- Publish consistently—once a week or biweekly—to build momentum and search rankings.
- Include calls-to-action at the end of each post: "Learn more," "Try our product," "Join our newsletter."

Influencer Outreach

- Collaborate with wellness influencers, herbalists, skincare bloggers, or sustainability advocates.
- Provide education-based content for them to share (vs. sales-driven material).
- Look for micro-influencers (1k–10k followers) with niche audiences and high engagement.
- Always vet influencers for credibility and alignment with your values.
- Use affiliate links or discount codes to track performance and incentivize sharing.

Influencer content often escapes algorithm suppression and reaches real people through trusted voices.

Building Private Communities and Safe Funnels

As public advertising becomes more restricted, private ecosystems are growing in popularity. These include subscriber-only email series, Discord servers, private Facebook Groups, and members-only learning hubs.

Private Community Examples:

- A "Hemp Wellness Circle" on Facebook with content, Q&As, and peer support
- A Discord server where you share behind-the-scenes content, product education, and lifestyle tips
- A subscription-only blog or video vault hosted on your site or a platform like Mighty Networks

Why they work:

- Members self-select to join, meaning they're already engaged.
- You avoid public content moderation and restrictions.
- You can build deeper relationships, generate user-generated content, and test new ideas safely.

Creating Safe Funnels:

- Use "neutral" lead magnets to collect emails (e.g., "The Herbal Wellness Starter Guide").
- Drive traffic to blog posts that contain subtle opt-ins, not sales copy.
- Route readers through nurturing email sequences before introducing products.

The key is subtlety, education, and value first. Sales will follow when trust is built.

Leveraging YouTube, Podcasts, and Alt-Tech Platforms

Alternative and long-form content channels offer massive visibility without the restrictions found on social media ads.

YouTube

- Create educational videos like "Hemp vs. CBD Explained," "How Hemp Supports Relaxation," or "What to Look for in a Quality Hemp Product."
- Include compliance-safe product showcases and behind-the-scenes content.
- Add timestamps, captions, and SEO-rich descriptions to boost ranking.
- Link to blog posts or email opt-ins—not direct store pages—in the video description.

Podcasts

- Start your own or appear on others. Share your expertise, values, and journey.
- Avoid direct product selling; focus on storytelling, industry insights, or customer success stories.
- Podcasts build deep emotional connection with highly loyal audiences.

Alt-Tech Platforms

- Explore Rumble, Odysee, and Substack for video or newsletter hosting without censorship.
- Use Brighteon or cannabis-friendly social platforms like Weed-Tube or Duby for niche targeting.
- Reddit and niche forums (e.g., Grasscity, Rollitup) offer high-trust engagement when used respectfully.

In a world where Big Tech limits your voice, *building your own media outlets and partnering with emerging platforms gives you freedom.*

Final Thoughts

Digital advertising in the hemp industry requires both strategy and agility. While major platforms may close doors, there are countless windows still open—and those windows reward creativity, authenticity, and education over hard selling.

Your goal isn't just to *run ads*—it's to build a digital ecosystem that attracts, nurtures, and converts your audience through valuable content and ethical communication. Every restricted policy is an invitation to innovate. Every barrier is a test of your brand's resilience.

Chapter 5: Content Marketing That Converts

Turning Education into Engagement—and Engagement into Sales

Content marketing isn't just about pumping out blogs or videos—it's about crafting a powerful narrative that educates, inspires, and gently guides your audience toward action. In the hemp industry, where skepticism, stigma, and legal constraints still loom large, content marketing becomes your most trustworthy bridge between awareness and purchase.

Whether you're selling CBD tinctures, hemp skincare, wellness kits, or industrial-grade products, the *right content* builds the *right kind of audience*—people who trust your voice, understand your values, and are more likely to become loyal customers.

This chapter explores how to harness storytelling, video, written content, and community participation to create a marketing ecosystem that not only informs but also converts.

The Role of Storytelling in Hemp Education

Storytelling is one of the most ancient and effective ways to educate. In an industry still fighting misinformation, your ability to wrap facts in emotion-rich narratives is critical.

Why Storytelling Works:

- Stories make complex topics relatable (e.g., explaining the endocannabinoid system through everyday experiences).
- They humanize your brand—especially when you share your origin story, mission, or customer experiences.
- They inspire action through empathy, not pressure.

Storytelling Ideas for Hemp Brands:

- **Your Founder Journey:** Share why you started your brand—did a personal health journey lead you to hemp? Were you inspired by sustainability? Let people see the real human behind the business.
- **Customer Success Stories:** Share real-life testimonials (with permission) from people who have benefitted from your products, being careful not to make unverified health claims.
- **The Product Lifecycle:** Show the journey from seed to shelf. Farmers, lab tests, packaging decisions—all help demystify hemp and build trust.
- **Problem-Solution Narratives:** "I was stressed. I tried everything. Then I found this one herbal remedy..."

Key Tip: The best storytelling isn't self-centered—it's customer-centered. Make the reader the hero of the journey.

Video Marketing Strategies for Visual Engagement

In today's digital world, video content reigns supreme. It's dynamic, emotionally rich, and far more engaging than static images or text alone. For hemp businesses, video is a non-negotiable part of a high-converting content strategy.

Types of Videos to Create:

1. **Educational Explainers**
   - "What Is Hemp?"
   - "How to Use Our CBD Balm for Better Sleep"
   - "The Science Behind Full-Spectrum Hemp"
2. **Behind-the-Scenes Footage**
   - Tours of your farm or production process
   - Interviews with staff, farmers, or formulators
   - Day-in-the-life reels that humanize your brand
3. **Customer Testimonials**
   - Invite customers to share how your product fits into their wellness routine
   - Make it natural, unscripted, and compliance-safe
4. **Product Demonstrations**
   - Show how to apply, cook with, or integrate the product into daily life

Best Practices for Video Marketing:

- Keep intro hooks under 3 seconds—especially for platforms like TikTok or Instagram Reels.
- Include captions for silent viewing.
- Use storytelling structure: Hook → Problem → Solution → Call-to-Action.
- Include CTA overlays ("Visit our site," "Learn more," "Download the guide").

Video increases conversion rates because it builds *emotional resonance* and helps overcome buyer hesitation by simulating real-life interaction.

Writing Informative Articles and How-To Guides
Educational content in article form is critical for SEO and consumer trust. Informative blog posts and how-to guides help attract organic traffic and position you as an authority.

High-Performing Article Formats:

- **How-To Guides:**
    - "How to Use Hemp Oil for Relaxation"
    - "How to Incorporate CBD Into Your Morning Routine"
- **Explainer Posts:**
    - "Hemp vs. Marijuana: What's the Difference?"
    - "What Is the Entourage Effect?"
- **Listicles:**
    - "7 Surprising Benefits of Hemp Skincare"
    - "5 Ways Hemp Helps the Environment"
- **Myth-Busting Articles:**
    - "No, Hemp Won't Get You High—Here's Why"
    - "The Truth About CBD and Drug Tests"

Best Practices for Written Content:

- Keep it skimmable with headings, subheadings, and bullet points.
- Use plain language and avoid jargon unless you're writing for a scientific audience.
- Include internal links to product pages or related articles.
- Always end with a CTA—ask the reader to subscribe, download, or explore your shop.

When well-written, articles don't just rank on Google—they act as quiet salespeople who work 24/7.

Encouraging User-Generated Content (UGC)

User-generated content is marketing gold. It's authentic, free, and persuasive. In the hemp industry, where brand trust is essential, UGC can dramatically boost your credibility.

What Counts as UGC:

- Instagram photos of customers using your products
- YouTube unboxing or review videos
- Blog posts written by happy customers
- Testimonials on your website or review platforms
- Social media comments or tags praising your brand

How to Encourage UGC:

- Create branded hashtags (e.g., #HempLifeWith[YourBrand])
- Run photo contests or giveaways ("Tag us for a chance to win")
- Feature customer content on your feed or in newsletters
- Offer discounts in exchange for reviews or testimonials
- Build a referral program or ambassador team

Always get consent before republishing someone's content. Make your customers feel like *part of the brand*, not just buyers.

Crafting an Editorial Calendar for Consistency

A solid editorial calendar ensures that your content marketing efforts stay consistent, purposeful, and aligned with your brand's goals.

Why It Matters:

- Prevents last-minute scrambling or creative burnout
- Ensures content is seasonally relevant (e.g., holiday gift guides, spring detox)
- Helps you track themes, formats, and engagement trends

What to Include in Your Editorial Calendar:

- **Date** and publishing frequency (e.g., every Tuesday)
- **Content Type** (blog post, video, email, infographic)
- **Topic/Title** (based on keyword research or seasonal trends)
- **Target Audience Segment** (e.g., new subscribers, loyal customers, beginners)
- **Distribution Channels** (blog, YouTube, email, social)
- **Assigned Creator** (yourself or team members)
- **CTA** and conversion goal (click, download, share, buy)

Use tools like Trello, Asana, Notion, or even Google Sheets to manage your calendar and track progress.

Monthly Editorial Focus Examples:

- **January:** "New Year, New You" hemp wellness series
- **April:** "Eco-Conscious Hemp for Earth Month"
- **July:** "Summer Stress Relief with Hemp Essentials"
- **November:** "Hemp Gifting Guide for the Holidays"

Planning ahead frees up your energy to create content that is not only high quality—but strategic and seasonally smart.

Final Thoughts

Content marketing for hemp is more than a workaround—it's a **superpower**. It allows you to bypass restrictive ad networks, educate your audience, and build loyalty through value, not gimmicks.

By integrating educational storytelling, persuasive writing, engaging videos, and authentic community content into a consistent publishing schedule, you'll grow a brand that doesn't just *sell*—it *leads*.

Content builds momentum. Momentum builds trust. Trust builds conversions.

Chapter 6: Traditional Marketing Channels That Still Work

Building Brand Awareness in the Physical World

While the digital landscape continues to expand, there is immense value in turning attention back to the physical world. In the hemp industry—where online advertising is heavily restricted—**traditional marketing channels** remain a vital, often underutilized, strategy for building brand awareness, reaching new audiences, and reinforcing credibility. From print ads and mailers to event sponsorships and billboards, these "old-school" tactics still work, especially when executed with modern strategy and design.

This chapter dives deep into how to effectively harness traditional marketing methods, legal concerns to watch out for, and how to seamlessly connect your offline efforts with your online presence to create a unified, memorable brand experience.

Print Ads in Niche Magazines and Local Newspapers

Print is far from dead—especially in niche and regional markets where your audience is highly targeted and engaged. Whether it's a holistic living magazine, a local newspaper, or a hemp-industry journal, print advertising offers a sense of credibility and permanence that digital sometimes lacks.

Where to Advertise:

- **Wellness & Alternative Health Magazines**
  (e.g., *Mind Body Green, Healing Springs Journal*)
- **Cannabis & Hemp Trade Publications**
  (e.g., *Hemp Grower, Cannabis Business Times*)
- **Local Community Newspapers**
  Ideal for promoting dispensaries, events, or educational workshops.

Tips for Effective Print Advertising:

- Use high-resolution, visually appealing design.
- Include a clear call-to-action (CTA), such as a QR code linking to your shop or newsletter.
- Highlight product benefits, but avoid any unapproved medical claims.
- Offer limited-time promotions or coupon codes to measure ad effectiveness.
- Place ads alongside relevant editorial content, such as wellness or sustainability features.

Print lends your brand a sense of professionalism and trustworthiness that digital alone may not always convey—especially to audiences over 40 who still read print regularly.

Direct Mail Campaigns and Product Sampling

Direct mail is making a comeback—especially in industries like hemp where online advertising can be blocked or throttled. Sending high-quality, branded materials directly to a customer's mailbox creates a tactile, memorable experience that stands out in a digital world.

Types of Direct Mail Campaigns:

- **Postcards** with product features, discounts, or educational facts
- **Brochures or Mini Catalogs** highlighting your best-selling items
- **Welcome Kits** with hemp education guides for new subscribers
- **Sample Packages** of non-ingestible products (like topicals or aromatherapy items)

Why Direct Mail Works:

- 42% of direct mail recipients read or scan the mail they receive.
- Physical materials have higher memory retention and longer shelf life.
- It bypasses ad blockers, algorithm limits, and digital overwhelm.

Best Practices:

- Personalize whenever possible (e.g., use the recipient's name).
- Use environmentally friendly, recyclable materials to align with hemp's sustainability values.
- Always include a tracking method (promo code, QR code, or short URL).

Sampling is especially powerful: giving customers a tactile or sensory experience with your product builds emotional trust and can lead to long-term loyalty.

Billboards, Flyers, and Event Sponsorships

Hemp brands can make a bold statement in public spaces—*if done correctly and legally*. Out-of-home advertising can be incredibly impactful when used in local markets or during strategic seasonal campaigns.

Billboards

- Best used for brand awareness, not sales.
- Strategically place near wellness clinics, holistic health centers, or farmer's markets.
- Avoid claims that could be flagged by regulators—focus on identity, lifestyle, and curiosity.
- Include short, bold messaging and a simple CTA (e.g., "Breathe Better. Live Naturally. Visit [YourBrand].com").

Flyers & Posters

- Use in local co-ops, yoga studios, health food stores, and cafes (with permission).
- Highlight educational content ("Hemp & You: The 5 Facts Everyone Should Know").
- Keep visuals clean and professional—avoid loud, cluttered designs.

Event Sponsorships

- Sponsor wellness festivals, sustainability expos, local farmers' markets, or cannabis-themed conventions.
- Offer giveaways, free samples (where legally allowed), or educational material at your booth.
- Collect email signups on-site using tablets, paper forms, or QR codes.
- Consider hosting your own "Hemp Wellness Day" or workshop series.

Tip: When your brand appears in the real world—especially in environments of trust and community—it gains a kind of legitimacy digital channels often struggle to replicate.

Legal Considerations for Traditional Media Placements

Marketing hemp in public spaces still requires careful attention to legality. Traditional outlets like newspapers, billboards, and sponsorships may have internal rules or legal guidelines you must follow.

Common Legal Restrictions:

- **No health claims.** Avoid any suggestion your product treats, cures, or prevents disease.
- **Age targeting:** Avoid advertising in spaces predominantly frequented by minors (e.g., school zones, children's events).
- **Labeling compliance:** Ensure any product images reflect your actual packaging, disclaimers, and legal requirements.
- **Local ordinances:** Check with city or county governments for signage restrictions, flyer regulations, or event requirements.
- **Third-party policies:** Print magazines or billboard companies may have their own internal restrictions about hemp-related content—even if it's legal.

Staying Safe:

- Use general wellness language instead of product-specific claims.
- Have a legal advisor review your ad copy before publication or installation.
- Include disclaimers where appropriate: "Not evaluated by the FDA," "For external use only," etc.

Every piece of advertising is a legal document. Treat it as such.

Integrating Offline and Online Branding

The most powerful brands create a **seamless experience across all channels.** Whether someone sees your flyer at a farmer's market or visits your blog online, the look, tone, and message should be instantly recognizable and cohesive.

Tips for Integrated Branding:

- Use consistent logos, fonts, and color schemes across print and digital.
- Mirror CTAs from offline materials in your digital campaigns (e.g., QR code → same landing page as email campaign).
- Promote offline events online, and vice versa.
- Include social media handles on physical materials.
- Cross-promote user-generated content from events or sponsorships onto your site and email newsletters.

Example Flow:

A customer sees your hemp booth at a wellness expo → takes home a branded flyer with a discount → scans the QR code → signs up for your newsletter → receives an automated welcome sequence → becomes a loyal buyer.

When offline and online work together, your marketing becomes omnipresent, trustworthy, and memorable.

Final Thoughts

Traditional marketing is not outdated—it's *underrated*. In a digital world flooded with pixels, notifications, and algorithmic noise, physical touchpoints cut through the chaos with sincerity and substance.

For hemp brands restricted by online ads, traditional marketing offers an essential pathway for visibility, trust, and local loyalty. Use these tools to supplement your digital strategy—not replace it—and you'll create a well-rounded, legally sound, and deeply resonant brand presence.

Chapter 7: Building a Hemp-Centered Community

From Transactional Customers to Transformational Advocates

In today's saturated hemp marketplace, the most successful brands are not the ones with the flashiest products or even the biggest budgets—they're the ones with the strongest **communities**. While many businesses focus on conversion metrics and ad campaigns, hemp entrepreneurs who focus on *connection* find themselves with something far more valuable: loyal customers who become passionate brand advocates.

Community is more than just a buzzword. It's the emotional infrastructure that keeps people coming back. A hemp-centered community creates trust in a misunderstood industry, nurtures repeat buyers, amplifies your message organically, and provides real-time insights into your customers' needs.

This chapter explores how to build and nurture a thriving community around your hemp brand—from live events to feedback loops—and how education becomes the root system that holds it all together.

Cultivating Loyal Customers and Brand Advocates

Loyal customers are your brand's best marketers. When nurtured properly, they don't just buy—they spread the word, leave reviews, and defend your brand against misinformation.

How to Build Loyalty in the Hemp Space:

1. **Deliver Consistency:**
   Trust starts with reliable product quality, fast shipping, responsive customer service, and consistent messaging.

2. **Reward Repeat Buyers:**
   - Offer loyalty programs with point systems or early access to new releases.
   - Give surprise gifts (samples, stickers, exclusive content) with large orders.
   - Create a VIP or subscription tier with added perks.

3. **Personalize Interactions:**
   - Use customer names in emails.
   - Tailor product recommendations based on purchase history.
   - Send birthday or "member since" thank-you notes.

4. **Celebrate Customer Stories:**
   Feature user testimonials, wellness journeys, or lifestyle photos on your blog and social media. Let your customers *see themselves* in your brand.

5. **Respond and Engage Proactively:**
   Be active in the comments, respond to DMs, and treat every review—good or bad—as an opportunity to show you care.

Your goal: **Turn transactions into trust, and trust into advocacy.**

Hosting Live Workshops and Virtual Q&As

Nothing builds community faster than real-time, interactive experiences. Live events—whether in-person or online—break down the walls between business and audience, creating human-to-human connection in an industry where trust is everything.

Types of Events to Host:

1. **Educational Workshops**
   - "Hemp 101: What You Need to Know"
   - "How to Use CBD in Your Wellness Routine"
   - "Sustainable Living with Hemp Products"

2. **Virtual Q&As**
   - Invite customers to ask anything about your products, sourcing, benefits, or legal questions.
   - Feature guest experts like herbalists, scientists, or holistic practitioners.

3. **Product Launch Parties**
   - Give sneak previews of upcoming products.
   - Offer exclusive discounts for attendees.
   - Gather instant feedback through polls or surveys.

4. **Community Rituals**
   - Guided meditations, moon-circle events, or stress-relief sessions using your products.

Event Best Practices:

- Promote the event across your email, social, and website at least 1–2 weeks in advance.
- Use tools like Zoom, Instagram Live, or Crowdcast for virtual events.
- Follow up with a thank-you email and exclusive post-event content or discount.

- Record the event and repurpose it for YouTube, blog content, or onboarding sequences.

These events deepen customer intimacy, build brand transparency, and establish your business as a trusted, interactive source of knowledge.

Creating Your Own Forums and Facebook Groups

When you create a *digital space* where your community can gather, you do more than sell—you start conversations, build connection, and gain insight into what your customers care about.

Benefits of Owning a Community Space:

- Full control over the conversation (vs. rented social media space).
- Ongoing, user-generated content and questions.
- Direct customer insights for product development or marketing language.
- Reduced dependence on paid ads for engagement.

Where to Build It:

- **Facebook Groups:** Easy to create, moderate, and grow using existing social media following.
- **Discord Servers:** Great for real-time chat, multiple topic channels, and deeper engagement.
- **Mighty Networks or Circle:** Paid platforms for creating branded communities with events, content, and courses.

Group Ideas:

- "The Hemp Wellness Circle" – A private group to share routines, ask questions, and explore hemp education.
- "Green Entrepreneurs Hub" – A business-to-business forum for hemp professionals and product creators.
- "CBD Moms & Dads" – A space for family-focused consumers to discuss stress relief, routines, and wellness.

Pro tip: Keep your groups active by regularly asking questions, hosting weekly live sessions, or sharing behind-the-scenes updates.

Collecting Feedback and Testimonials

Feedback is the fuel of continuous improvement and proof of trust. It also serves as social proof—a key driver in customer decision-making.

How to Collect It Effectively:

1. **After-Purchase Surveys:**
   Use email automation to ask for feedback 7–10 days after delivery.
2. **Incentivized Reviews:**
   Offer small rewards or future discounts in exchange for honest reviews.
3. **Live Feedback During Events:**
   Use polls and open Q&A sessions to hear real-time responses to new products or ideas.
4. **Testimonial Campaigns:**
   Invite your best customers to submit stories, photos, or video testimonials in exchange for store credit or exclusive perks.

What to Do With It:

- Publish it across your product pages, home page, social posts, and sales emails.
- Address recurring feedback themes to improve packaging, labeling, or communication.
- Use positive testimonials in *retargeting* or email campaigns.
- Turn questions into content ideas (e.g., "Top 5 Customer Questions About Our Balm").

Feedback helps you *see what your customers see*—and improve accordingly.

Education as a Branding Strategy

In the hemp space, *education isn't optional—it's essential.* Unlike other wellness products, hemp still faces skepticism, stigma, and confusion. Brands that step up to teach become the most trusted, followed, and respected in the industry.

Why Education Builds Brand Power:

- It builds trust in an industry filled with misinformation.
- It positions your brand as an authority.
- It drives organic search traffic and referrals.
- It empowers your audience to make informed buying decisions—reducing friction.

Ways to Integrate Education:

- **Blog Articles:** Regular, SEO-optimized content covering hemp benefits, how-tos, legality, and sourcing.
- **Infographics:** Visual breakdowns of how hemp works, how to read lab results, or how CBD affects the body.
- **Short-form Videos:** TikTok, Instagram Reels, and YouTube Shorts that answer one question per video.
- **Mini-Courses:** Email drip campaigns or website courses on hemp wellness, skincare, or sustainability.
- **PDF Guides & Downloads:** Offer eBooks like "The Beginner's Guide to CBD" or "How to Read a Hemp Label" in exchange for email signups.

Your educational content becomes the *entry point* to your community—and the bridge between confusion and confidence for potential customers.

Final Thoughts

Community is the heartbeat of every thriving hemp brand. It's what transforms a faceless transaction into a trusted relationship. In a world where algorithms shift and ad platforms ban keywords, **your people will always be your strongest asset**.

Invest in them. Speak to them. Build for them.

A hemp-centered community isn't just good for business—it's good for the soul of your brand.

Chapter 8: Data Analytics and Measuring Success

Transforming Numbers into Strategic Growth for Your Hemp Business

In the hemp industry, success doesn't happen by accident—it's measured, tracked, and refined. With advertising restrictions and evolving regulations limiting traditional marketing paths, hemp brands must be especially strategic. That's where data analytics becomes essential. It helps you understand what works, what doesn't, and how to fine-tune your efforts for better outcomes—without wasting time, money, or momentum.

Whether you're running an online store, a virtual dispensary, or offering educational content, data gives you clarity. In this chapter, we'll explore how to set meaningful marketing goals, use the right tools to track performance, evaluate user behavior, and continuously improve based on the feedback and insights you gather.

Setting Key Performance Indicators (KPIs)

Key Performance Indicators (KPIs) are specific, measurable goals that help you assess whether your marketing and business strategies are effective. Without them, you're essentially working in the dark.

KPIs give you direction. They reveal what's gaining traction and where adjustments are needed. For hemp businesses, they are especially important because they allow you to adapt quickly in a space where rules change fast and ad access is limited.

Examples of KPIs to Track:

- **Website Traffic:** The number of visitors to your site. A growing number indicates that your outreach and visibility efforts are working.
- **Conversion Rate:** The percentage of visitors who take an action—like buying a product, signing up for your newsletter, or downloading a guide.
- **Email Open and Click-Through Rates:** These tell you how engaging your email campaigns are and whether your messaging resonates.
- **Customer Acquisition Cost:** How much you're spending to bring in each new customer. This helps determine if your efforts are cost-effective.
- **Customer Retention Rate:** The percentage of returning customers. High retention means your brand is building trust and satisfaction.
- **Average Order Value:** How much a customer typically spends per transaction. This number can guide bundling and upsell strategies.

Start with a handful of KPIs that reflect your goals—such as increasing conversions, boosting engagement, or reducing acquisition costs—and track them consistently.

Tools for Tracking Traffic, Conversions, and ROI

To gather and analyze data effectively, you need reliable tools that provide clear, actionable insights. Fortunately, there are several platforms—many of them free or affordable—that can help you understand how people interact with your brand.

Key Tools to Use:

- **Google Analytics:** Offers deep insights into your website traffic, user behavior, and where visitors are coming from. It shows how long they stay, which pages they visit, and what actions they take.
- **Google Search Console:** Helps you understand how your site is performing in search engines. You can see which keywords are bringing in traffic and how often people are clicking on your links.
- **Shopify or WooCommerce Dashboards:** These ecommerce platforms provide sales data, product performance, and customer behavior analytics all in one place.
- **Email Marketing Platforms (like Mailchimp, Klaviyo, or ConvertKit):** These services show how many people open your emails, click links, unsubscribe, or make a purchase after receiving a message.
- **Social Media Analytics:** Platforms like Instagram, Facebook, and YouTube offer built-in insights into engagement, reach, and audience growth.

Use these tools regularly—not just after campaigns, but weekly or monthly—to monitor your performance trends and spot opportunities or weaknesses early.

Using Heatmaps, Surveys, and A/B Testing

Beyond the numbers, understanding how users *feel* and *behave* on your site or with your content can offer rich insights that lead to better decisions.

Heatmaps

Heatmaps visually display where people are clicking, scrolling, or hovering on your website. They reveal which parts of your pages attract attention—and which areas are ignored.

- If people aren't clicking on your main "Buy Now" button, it might need to be more prominent.
- If they scroll only halfway down your homepage, you may need to move key information higher.

Tools like Hotjar and Crazy Egg help you capture these interactions and make layout changes that can significantly boost conversions.

Surveys

Surveys allow you to gather feedback directly from your audience. This can be done through pop-ups, email follow-ups, or thank-you pages after a purchase.

Questions to ask:

- "What made you decide to buy from us?"
- "What almost stopped you from completing your order?"
- "What kind of hemp content or products would you like to see next?"

Even a few thoughtful responses can reveal patterns that lead to better copywriting, more effective offers, or smarter product development.

A/B Testing

A/B testing is when you compare two versions of something—like a headline, email subject, or homepage layout—to see which one performs better.

- Change just one element at a time.
- Test it with a large enough audience to gather meaningful results.
- Measure which version gets more clicks, sales, or signups.

Over time, testing helps you refine your message, design, and customer journey for maximum impact.

Understanding Customer Lifetime Value (CLTV)

Customer Lifetime Value (CLTV) is a powerful metric that helps you understand how much a single customer is worth to your business over time—not just from their first purchase, but across all future transactions.

Why it matters:

- It helps you budget better for marketing and retention.
- It identifies your most valuable customer segments.
- It allows you to prioritize nurturing long-term relationships.

Increasing CLTV

You can raise a customer's lifetime value by:

- Offering subscriptions or memberships for recurring revenue.
- Upselling and cross-selling related products.
- Creating loyalty rewards or exclusive content.
- Sending personalized product recommendations based on past purchases.

When you understand CLTV, you can shift your focus from one-time sales to building long-term trust—and that's where real growth happens.

Optimizing Based on Feedback and Engagement

Gathering data is only half the battle. The real power lies in acting on what you've learned.

How to Optimize:

1. **Review Your KPIs Regularly:**
   Don't just check stats after launching something new. Establish a routine—weekly or monthly reviews—to evaluate performance.

2. **Fix What's Not Working:**
   If a landing page has lots of traffic but few conversions, improve the call-to-action or product descriptions. If email open rates drop, experiment with subject lines or send times.

3. **Double Down on What Works:**
   If a certain blog post brings in a lot of traffic, create more content on that topic. If a product bundle sells well, promote it in your emails and ads.

4. **Listen Closely to Customers:**
   Use their testimonials, complaints, and suggestions to improve your messaging, products, and processes. They are your best source of real-world insight.

5. **Integrate Insights Across Your Team:**
   Share what you learn with everyone involved in your business—from customer service to product development—so your entire operation grows smarter together.

Feedback and engagement are your business's compass. They tell you what your audience values and where they want you to go next.

Final Thoughts

Analytics isn't just about charts and dashboards—it's about **understanding people** and **making better decisions**. In a restrictive advertising environment like hemp, smart use of data can be your competitive edge.

By setting meaningful goals, tracking your performance with the right tools, and continually adjusting your strategy based on what works, you'll build a hemp brand that not only survives but thrives—grounded in clarity, confidence, and continual growth.

Chapter 9: Navigating Obstacles and Censorship

Thriving Amid Suppression, Restrictions, and the Shifting Rules of the Game

For hemp businesses, censorship is not just a theoretical concern—it's a daily reality. Despite federal legalization of hemp under the 2018 Farm Bill, platforms like Facebook, Instagram, Google, and Tik-Tok continue to impose restrictions that treat hemp products like illicit substances. From shadowbans and content takedowns to outright ad rejections, entrepreneurs often find themselves unfairly silenced, penalized, or invisible.

But navigating this minefield is not only possible—it's survivable, and even conquerable. Brands that endure don't rely on permission from big platforms. They build resilience through creative strategies, legal knowledge, and a flexible marketing mindset.

In this chapter, we'll explore how to understand and respond to censorship, navigate penalties, harness third-party channels, and create a long-term brand strategy that doesn't depend on any single algorithm, platform, or policy.

Coping with Shadowbans and Flagged Content

A **shadowban** occurs when your content is restricted or hidden by a platform's algorithm—*without notification*. Your followers may stop seeing your posts, your engagement might drop, and new users may struggle to find you—even though your account hasn't technically violated any rules.

Signs You've Been Shadowbanned:

- Sudden drop in views, reach, or engagement despite consistent content
- Hashtags no longer driving traffic to your posts
- Posts not showing up in follower feeds
- Content removed without specific reasons

What to Do About It:

1. **Pause Promotion of Restricted Terms**
   Avoid using flagged words like "CBD," "cannabis," "hemp oil," "THC," or "pain relief." Use education-based language or indirect phrasing instead (e.g., "plant-based wellness," "green ritual").

2. **Switch Up Your Content Format**
   Use carousels, videos, and live streams instead of static posts. Different formats may be treated more favorably by platform algorithms.

3. **Clean Your Hashtags**
   Avoid banned or flagged hashtags and rotate your tag sets regularly. Reusing the same set repeatedly may trigger suspicion.

4. **Engage Like a Human**
   Respond to comments, share stories, and avoid spammy behavior like rapid mass-following or auto-commenting.

5. **Diversify Your Channels**
   Don't rely solely on one platform. Spread your brand across

email, YouTube, podcasts, alt-tech platforms, and your own website.

Remember: shadowbanning is not a permanent ban—it's an opportunity to reevaluate and adapt.

Appealing Ad Rejections and Platform Penalties

Hemp entrepreneurs face repeated ad rejections—even when they follow the rules. Understanding how to appeal—and when to pivot—is key.

Steps for Appealing Rejected Ads:

1. **Review the Platform's Ad Policies Thoroughly**
   Each platform has its own restrictions. Some ban CBD entirely; others allow topicals with strict disclaimers.

2. **Check the Language in Your Ad**
   Remove or reword any references to CBD, medical benefits, or body-specific results (like "relieves pain" or "treats anxiety"). Use phrases like "supports wellness" or "plant-based recovery."

3. **Use Compliant Imagery**
   Avoid showing products with dosage information, lab results, or people consuming them.

4. **Submit an Appeal**
   Platforms like Meta and Google have an appeal button on rejected ads. Explain clearly why your ad complies and what language you've removed.

5. **Provide Documentation if Requested**
   For hemp topicals, provide proof of product legality and third-party testing.

6. **Create Separate Landing Pages for Ads**
   Redirect ads to general brand pages or educational resources instead of product pages that trigger restrictions.

If Penalties Escalate:

- Request a manual review of your account.
- Create a second, backup business page as a safeguard.
- Consider running *adjacent* campaigns (wellness, lifestyle, sustainability) rather than direct product promotions.

If your account is permanently banned, it's critical to have already built a customer base outside that platform.

Using Affiliate Networks and Third-Party Marketplaces

When you can't promote your product directly, let *others* do it for you.

Affiliate marketing and alternative marketplaces provide indirect promotional power—especially when your primary channels are restricted.

Affiliate Marketing:

- Recruit influencers, bloggers, or micro-creators to promote your products through affiliate links.
- Offer a generous commission structure (typically 10–30% per sale).
- Use platforms like ShareASale, Refersion, or GoAffPro to track sales and manage payouts.

Benefits:

- Builds organic, trust-based referrals.
- Spreads your brand across multiple audiences.
- Keeps you in compliance by decentralizing promotional messaging.

Third-Party Marketplaces:

- **Hemp-specific platforms:** Leafly, Weedmaps, The CBDistillery Marketplace
- **Wellness eCommerce sites:** Thrive Market, Green Wellness Life
- **Subscription boxes:** Partner with brands like Cure Crate or Hemp Crate Co.

Note: Ensure your products are accurately labeled and comply with the guidelines of each third-party site.

These platforms already have warm traffic, compliance teams, and search authority—making it easier for you to scale visibility while avoiding censorship.

Legal Routes to Challenge or Reframe Compliance Rules

If you feel a platform or service provider has unfairly penalized your hemp business, you have legal and procedural avenues to push back.

What You Can Do:

1. **Document Everything**
   Save emails, screenshots, appeal correspondence, and rejections.
2. **Consult a Cannabis or Hemp Law Attorney**
   Some firms specialize in fighting platform bias, payment processor bans, or vague language in terms of service.
3. **File a Business Complaint**
   You can submit formal complaints to:
   - The Better Business Bureau (BBB)
   - State attorney general's office
   - FTC (if misleading policies or anti-competitive behavior is suspected)
4. **Request Clarification in Writing**
   If you're using a fulfillment provider, bank, or ad platform that restricts you, ask for a written policy so you can tailor your approach accordingly.
5. **Join Industry Advocacy Groups**
   Organizations like the National Hemp Association and U.S. Hemp Roundtable work to challenge unfair laws and promote reform. Being part of these groups gives you a voice in shaping the legal landscape.

While legal processes can be slow, your brand should always be aligned with what is **defensible, documented, and ethical.**

Building Marketing Resilience and Flexibility

The future of hemp marketing will always be in flux. The smartest brands prepare not just for growth—but for disruption.

Principles of Resilient Hemp Marketing:

1. **Own Your Audience**
   - Build and nurture an email list.
   - Create downloadable content, memberships, or communities to stay in contact if platforms go dark.

2. **Diversify Your Channels**
   - Don't rely on one platform. Use a mix of:
     - Website
     - Email
     - YouTube
     - LinkedIn
     - Discord
     - Podcasts
     - Influencer networks

3. **Create Content That Educates**
   - Educational content is harder to censor than product pitches.
   - Focus on wellness routines, sustainability, industry news, and customer success stories.

4. **Invest in Owned Platforms**
   - Build a blog.
   - Develop your own app or learning portal.
   - Host videos on platforms like Rumble or Vimeo.

5. **Have a "Platform Exit Plan"**
   - If your Instagram is deleted tomorrow, how will your followers find you?
   - Make sure your audience knows how to join your email list or community.

Flexibility is not just a strength—it's a survival strategy. Resilient brands anticipate change, adapt quickly, and never put all their marketing power in one basket.

Final Thoughts

Censorship and obstacles are part of the hemp journey. But they're not roadblocks—they're *redirections*. They force you to think smarter, create stronger content, and build brands that don't depend on one algorithm or advertising loophole.

You don't need to scream louder to be heard—you need to build relationships, educate authentically, and outlast the noise.

Chapter 10: The Future of Hemp Marketing

Vision, Innovation, and Staying Ahead in a Transforming Industry

As the hemp industry matures, it is no longer defined solely by novelty or controversy. It is transforming into a permanent fixture of wellness, sustainability, and global commerce. With this shift comes a crucial question for entrepreneurs and marketers: *What's next?*

Hemp marketing is entering a new era—one shaped by evolving technologies, stricter (and smarter) regulations, environmentally conscious consumers, and an increased reliance on automation. To thrive in this future, brands must be visionary and agile, willing to evolve while staying rooted in transparency, education, and purpose.

In this final chapter, we'll explore key trends that are already reshaping the landscape and what actions you can take today to remain competitive, compliant, and compelling in the years to come.

Emerging Trends in Hemp Technology and Advertising

New innovations are pushing the boundaries of what hemp brands can achieve—not just in product formulation, but in how they reach, educate, and serve customers.

Trends to Watch:

1. **Nano-Delivery Systems**
   Advanced formulations allow hemp extracts (especially CBD and CBG) to be absorbed faster and more effectively. Marketers will need to simplify these concepts for consumer understanding without making unapproved medical claims.

2. **Blockchain for Transparency**
   Some hemp brands are adopting blockchain to track product origins, lab testing, and production processes. Transparent labeling backed by verifiable data builds unmatched trust in a skeptical market.

3. **Augmented Reality (AR) Shopping**
   Virtual try-ons, interactive packaging, and 3D product demos help eCommerce stores stand out while enhancing buyer confidence. AR is expected to grow significantly as consumer attention shifts to immersive experiences.

4. **Voice Search Optimization**
   With more people using Alexa, Siri, and Google Assistant, optimizing content for voice search ("Where can I buy organic hemp lotion?") will be essential for discoverability.

5. **Decentralized Advertising**
   Brands are exploring Web3-based platforms, token-based rewards, and independent ad networks to bypass centralized censorship and build direct, peer-driven customer relationships.

As these technologies become mainstream, hemp marketers must pair innovation with education—translating complexity into clarity for everyday consumers.

Sustainability as a Branding Strategy

Consumers today want more than a great product—they want to support companies that align with their values. Sustainability is no longer a niche—it's a *competitive advantage*, especially in the hemp space, where eco-conscious farming and production are already core strengths.

Make Sustainability Visible in Your Brand Story:

- **Highlight Carbon-Neutral Practices**
  Whether it's regenerative agriculture or biodegradable packaging, tell your audience *how* your business minimizes environmental harm.
- **Use Certifications and Visual Symbols**
  USDA Organic, CarbonFree, or B Corp labels help reinforce your commitment to ethical practices.
- **Promote Circular Economy Products**
  Hemp fibers can be reused or composted. If your products or packaging are recyclable, reusable, or refillable—market that loudly.
- **Educate Through Content**
  Create blog posts, videos, and social media series around sustainability topics (e.g., "Why Hemp is the Future of Green Manufacturing").

Brands that demonstrate environmental responsibility are more likely to earn loyalty, partnerships, and long-term relevance—especially with Millennial and Gen Z consumers.

Forecasting Customer Demands and Legal Changes

The hemp industry's future depends on anticipating where both the market and the law are headed. Businesses that guess wrong may be forced to rebrand or pivot at great cost. Those who watch the signs can ride the wave.

Key Areas to Monitor:

1. **Consumer Sophistication**

   Early adopters of hemp were satisfied with basic products. Now, customers expect transparency, consistency, and education. They want to know:
   - What's in your product?
   - How does it work?
   - What makes it different from everyone else's?

2. **State and Federal Regulations**

   Some states are moving toward banning certain cannabinoids like Delta-8 THC. Others are creating stricter labeling requirements. Stay informed through:
   - Industry newsletters
   - Trade associations (e.g., U.S. Hemp Roundtable)
   - Legal advisors specializing in cannabis and hemp law

3. **Retail Channel Shifts**

   Traditional dispensaries may give way to health-focused retailers, spas, or subscription services. Think beyond "cannabis culture" and explore wellness, skincare, pet health, and fitness markets.

4. **Increased FDA Oversight**

   As consumer demand rises, the FDA is under pressure to create clearer frameworks for hemp-derived products. Expect updated guidance on labeling, claims, and testing.

Pro Tip: Build a brand flexible enough to shift messaging, reformulate products, or adjust your target demographic without losing your identity.

How AI and Automation Are Reshaping Outreach

The rise of AI is redefining what it means to run a lean, smart, and responsive business. For hemp marketers, automation doesn't mean replacing creativity—it means *amplifying it.*

Ways to Use AI and Automation Right Now:

1. **Email Personalization**
   Tools like Klaviyo and ActiveCampaign allow you to send custom messages based on customer behavior—such as abandoned carts, past purchases, or browsing history.
2. **AI Copywriting and Content Generation**
   Platforms like Jasper or ChatGPT can help you brainstorm blog ideas, generate product descriptions, or write educational content in seconds—allowing you to stay consistent with less effort.
3. **Chatbots and Customer Service Automation**
   AI-driven chat support can handle FAQs, direct users to helpful content, and collect leads—all while reducing staffing needs.
4. **Predictive Analytics**
   Platforms can now forecast product demand, identify customer drop-off points, and recommend inventory strategies based on historical data.
5. **Automated Social Media Scheduling**
   Plan posts weeks in advance across platforms with tools like Later, Buffer, or Hootsuite—keeping your messaging consistent even when you're not online.

Automation helps you scale outreach without burning out. The goal isn't to become robotic—it's to *free up more energy for authentic engagement and innovation.*

Staying Authentic in a Rapidly Evolving Industry

Trends change. Platforms come and go. But what remains constant is the human desire for truth, connection, and reliability. As competitors race to automate, expand, or outshout each other, authenticity becomes your strongest differentiator.

Keys to Remaining Authentic:

- **Tell Your Story Honestly**
  Share why you started, what challenges you've overcome, and who you're helping. Vulnerability breeds loyalty.
- **Respond to Real Feedback**
  Don't just promote products—engage with reviews, answer questions openly, and listen when people raise concerns.
- **Create Content That Serves**
  Focus on education, empowerment, and real value. Sales will follow trust.
- **Maintain Consistent Values**
  As you scale, hold true to your original mission. Don't chase trends that contradict your brand's ethics or voice.

Authenticity isn't a tactic—it's a long-term investment. It keeps your community intact even when the rules change, platforms shut down, or trends shift overnight.

Final Thoughts

The future of hemp marketing will belong to those who **stay informed, embrace innovation**, and **remain deeply human**. Whether you're navigating regulation, exploring AI, or scaling your message across new platforms, your success depends on your ability to blend *strategy with soul*.

Build your brand like the hemp plant itself—strong, versatile, and rooted in purpose. Because in the years ahead, it won't be the loudest voices or the trendiest brands that survive. It will be the most *adaptable*, *ethical*, and *authentic*.

This is only the beginning.
Your journey into the green frontier continues—beyond ads, beyond platforms, and into lasting impact.

Appendix A: Glossary of Key Terms

A Comprehensive Reference for Hemp Marketing and Industry Terminology

Understanding the language of the hemp industry is crucial for navigating its evolving landscape. Whether you're a new entrepreneur or a seasoned marketer, this glossary offers concise and clear definitions of essential terms that appear throughout this book. Use it as a reference guide to support strategic decisions, improve communication with your audience, and stay grounded in the terminology that drives modern hemp commerce.

Brand Identity

The complete visual and messaging system that defines a company's public image. This includes elements such as the logo, color palette, font choices, packaging style, brand voice, and tone—all of which contribute to how a brand is recognized and emotionally received by consumers.

CBD (Cannabidiol)

A naturally occurring compound found in hemp, CBD is a non-psychoactive cannabinoid known for its therapeutic potential. It is often used in wellness products to support relaxation, recovery, and general health, without producing a high.

Compliance

The process of ensuring all marketing, labeling, product formulation, and business practices follow applicable local, state, and federal laws. In the hemp industry, compliance often relates to THC thresholds, product claims, packaging, and advertising restrictions.

Content Marketing

A long-term marketing strategy that involves creating and distributing valuable, informative, and consistent content to attract and retain a clearly defined audience—ultimately driving profitable customer actions. Examples include blog articles, videos, infographics, guides, and podcasts.

Digital Marketing

The use of online channels—including social media, email, search engines, and websites—to promote products or services. For hemp brands, digital marketing often involves indirect strategies due to platform restrictions on cannabis-related content.

Endocannabinoid System (ECS)

A complex cell-signaling system in the human body that helps regulate mood, sleep, appetite, immune response, and more. It interacts with cannabinoids like CBD and THC, which bind to ECS receptors to produce various physiological effects.

Guerrilla Marketing

Unconventional, cost-effective marketing tactics that rely on creativity, boldness, and originality to generate buzz and maximize exposure. Examples include flash mobs, street art, pop-up experiences, and grassroots promotions—especially useful when traditional advertising is restricted.

Hemp

A specific variety of the Cannabis sativa plant cultivated for industrial, dietary, and therapeutic use. Legally defined in the U.S. as cannabis with less than 0.3% THC by dry weight, hemp is used to create textiles, building materials, oils, edibles, and supplements.

KPI (Key Performance Indicator)

A quantifiable metric used to evaluate the success of specific business objectives. In marketing, KPIs may include website traffic, conversion rate, customer retention, and return on ad spend—helping businesses measure and refine their strategies.

SEO (Search Engine Optimization)

A set of practices designed to increase a website's visibility in organic search results. Effective SEO includes keyword research, content optimization, backlink building, and technical improvements—ensuring that your site attracts traffic from users actively searching for relevant topics.

THC (Tetrahydrocannabinol)

The primary psychoactive compound in cannabis that causes a "high." In legal hemp products, the THC content must remain below the legal threshold of 0.3% by dry weight. Higher concentrations classify a product as marijuana, which remains federally illegal in the U.S.

USP (Unique Selling Proposition)

The specific benefit or feature that differentiates your product or brand from the competition. A strong USP clearly answers the customer's question: "Why should I choose this over something else?"

User-Generated Content (UGC)

Any form of content—such as social media posts, videos, testimonials, or reviews—created by consumers rather than the brand itself. UGC builds social proof and authenticity, often leading to increased engagement and trust among potential buyers.

This glossary is a living resource. As the hemp industry evolves, so too will the language used to describe its innovations, practices, and challenges. Revisit this appendix often to stay fluent in the terminology that empowers strategic growth and effective communication.

<u>**Message from the Author**</u>:

I hope you enjoyed this book, I love astrology and knew there was not a book such as this out on the shelf. I love metaphysical items as well. Please check out my other books:

-Life of Government Benefits

-My life of Hell

-My life with Hydrocephalus

-Red Sky

-World Domination:Woman's rule

-World Domination:Woman's Rule 2: The War

-Life and Banishment of Apophis: book 1

-The Kidney Friendly Diet

-The Ultimate Hemp Cookbook

-Creating a Dispensary(legally)

-Cleanliness throughout life: the importance of showering from childhood to adulthood.

-Strong Roots: The Risks of Overcoddling children

-Hemp Horoscopes: Cosmic Insights and Earthly Healing

- Celestial Hemp Navigating the Zodiac: Through the Green Cosmos

-Astrological Hemp: Aligning The Stars with Earth's Ancient Herb

-The Astrological Guide to Hemp: Stars, Signs, and Sacred Leaves

-Green Growth: Innovative Marketing Strategies for your Hemp Products and Dispensary

-Cosmic Cannabis

-Astrological Munchies

-Henry The Hemp

-Zodiacal Roots: The Astrological Soul Of Hemp

- **Green Constellations: Intersection of Hemp and Zodiac**

-Hemp in The Houses: An astrological Adventure Through The Cannabis Galaxy

-Galactic Ganja Guide

Heavenly Hemp
Zodiac Leaves
Doctor Who Astrology
Cannastrology
Stellar Satvias and Cosmic Indicas
Celestial Cannabis: A Zodiac Journey
AstroHerbology: The Sky and The Soil: Volume 1
AstroHerbology:Celestial Cannabis:Volume 2
Cosmic Cannabis Cultivation
The Starry Guide to Herbal Harmony: Volume 1
The Starry Guide to Herbal Harmony: Cannabis Universe: Volume 2

Yugioh Astrology: Astrological Guide to Deck, Duels and more
Nightmare Mansion: Echoes of The Abyss
Nightmare Mansion 2: Legacy of Shadows
Nightmare Mansion 3: Shadows of the Forgotten
Nightmare Mansion 4: Echoes of the Damned
The Life and Banishment of Apophis: Book 2
Nightmare Mansion: Halls of Despair
Healing with Herb: Cannabis and Hydrocephalus
Planetary Pot: Aligning with Astrological Herbs: Volume 1
Fast Track to Freedom: 30 Days to Financial Independence Using AI, Assets, and Agile Hustles
Cosmic Hemp Pathways
How to Become Financially Free in 30 Days: 10,000 Paths to Prosperity
Zodiacal Herbage: Astrological Insights: Volume 1
Nightmare Mansion: Whispers in the Walls
The Daleks Invade Atlantis
Henry the hemp and Hydrocephalus

10X The Kidney Friendly Diet
Cannabis Universe: Adult coloring book

Hemp Astrology: The Healing Power of the Stars

Zodiacal Herbage: Astrological Insights: Cannabis Universe: Volume 2

<u>**Planetary Pot: Aligning with Astrological Herbs: Cannabis Universes: Volume 2**</u>

Doctor Who: Convergence Protocol – The Replicator War

Nightmare Mansion: Curse of the Blood Moon

<u>**The Celestial Stoner: A Guide to the Zodiac**</u>

Cosmic Pleasures: Sex Toy Astrology for Every Sign

Hydrocephalus Astrology: Navigating the Stars and Healing Waters

Lapis and the Mischievous Chocolate Bar

Celestial Positions: Sexual Astrology for Every Sign

Apophis's Shadow Work Journal: : A Journey of Self-Discovery and Healing

Kinky Cosmos: Sexual Kink Astrology for Every Sign

Digital Cosmos: The Astrological Digimon Compendium

Stellar Seeds: The Cosmic Guide to Growing with Astrology

Apophis's Daily Gratitude Journal

Cat Astrology: Feline Mysteries of the Cosmos

The Cosmic Kama Sutra: An Astrological Guide to Sexual Positions

Unleash Your Potential: A Guided Journal Powered by AI Insights

Whispers of the Enchanted Grove

Cosmic Pleasures: An Astrological Guide to Sexual Kinks

369, 12 Manifestation Journal

Whisper of the nocturne journal(blank journal for writing or drawing)

The Boogey Book

Locked In Reflection: A Chastity Journey Through Locktober

Generating Wealth Quickly:How to Generate $100,000 in 24 Hours

Star Magic: Harness the Power of the Universe

The Flatulence Chronicles: A Fart Journal for Self-Discovery

The Doctor and The Death Moth

Seize the Day: A Personal Seizure Tracking Journal

The Ultimate Boogeyman Safari: A Journey into the Boogie World and Beyond

Whispers of Samhain: 1,000 Spells of Love, Luck, and Lunar Magic: Samhain Spell Book

Apophis's guides:Witch's Spellbook Crafting Guide for Halloween

<u>Frost & Flame: The Enchanted Yule Grimoire of 1000 Winter Spells</u>

<u>The Ultimate Boogey Goo Guide & Spooky Activities for Halloween Fun</u>

Harmony of the Scales: A Libra's Spellcraft for Balance and Beauty

The Enchanted Advent: 36 Days of Christmas Wonders

Nightmare Mansion: The Labyrinth of Screams

Harvest of Enchantment: 1,000 Spells of Gratitude, Love, and Fortune for Thanksgiving

The Boogey Chronicles: A Journal of Nightly Encounters and Shadowy Secrets

The 12 Days of Financial Freedom: A Step-by-Step Christmas Countdown to Transform Your Finances

Sigil of the Eternal Spiral Blank Journal

A Christmas Feast: Timeless Recipes for Every Meal

Holiday Stress-Free Solutions: A Survival Guide to Thriving During the Festive Season

Yu-Gi-Oh! Holiday Gifting Mastery: The Ultimate Guide for Fans and Newcomers Alike

Holiday Harmony: A Hydrocephalus Survival Guide for the Festive Season

Celestial Craft: The Witch's Almanac for 2025 – A Cosmic Guide to Manifestations, Moons, and Mystical Events

Doctor Who: The Toymaker's Winter Wonderland

Tulsa King Unveiled: A Thrilling Guide to Stallone's Mafia Masterpiece

Pendulum Craft: A Complete Guide to Crafting and Using Personalized Divination Tools

Nightmare Mansion: Santa's Eternal Eve

Starlight Noel: A Cosmic Journey through Christmas Mysteries

The Dark Architect: Unlocking the Blueprint of Existence

Surviving the Embrace: The Ultimate Guide to Encounters with The Hugging Molly

The Enchanted Codex: Secrets of the Craft for Witches, Wiccans, and Pagans

Harvest of Gratitude: A Complete Thanksgiving Guide

Yuletide Essentials: A Complete Guide to an Authentic and Magical Christmas

Celestial Smokes: A Cosmic Guide to Cigars and Astrology

Living in Balance: A Comprehensive Survival Guide to Thriving with Diabetes Insipidus

Cosmic Symbiosis: The Venom Zodiac Chronicles

The Cursed Paw of Ambition

Cosmic Symbiosis: The Astrological Venom Journal

Celestial Wonders Unfold: A Stargazer's Guide to the Cosmos (2024-2029)

The Ultimate Black Friday Prepper's Guide: Mastering Shopping Strategies and Savings

Cosmic Sales: The Astrological Guide to Black Friday Shopping

Legends of the Corn Mother and Other Harvest Myths

Whispers of the Harvest: The Corn Mother's Journal

The Evergreen Spellbook

The Doctor Meets the Boogeyman

The White Witch of Rose Hall's SpellBook

The Gingerbread Golem's Shadow: A Study in Sweet Darkness

The Gingerbread Golem Codex: An Academic Exploration of Sweet Myths

The Gingerbread Golem Grimoire: Sweet Magicks and Spells for the Festive Witch

The Curse of the Gingerbread Golem

10-minute Christmas Crafts for kids

<u>Christmas Crisis Solutions: The Ultimate Last-Minute Survival Guide</u>

Gingerbread Golem Recipes: Holiday Treats with a Magical Twist

The Infinite Key: Unlocking Mystical Secrets of the Ages

Enchanted Yule: A Wiccan and Pagan Guide to a Magical and Memorable Season

Dinosaurs of Power: Unlocking Ancient Magick

Astro-Dinos: The Cosmic Guide to Prehistoric Wisdom

Gallifrey's Yule Logs: A Festive Doctor Who Cookbook

The Dino Grimoire: Secrets of Prehistoric Magick

The Gift They Never Knew They Needed

The Gingerbread Golem's Culinary Alchemy: Enchanting Recipes for a Sweetly Dark Feast

A Time Lord Christmas: Holiday Adventures with the Doctor

Krampusproofing Your Home: Defensive Strategies for Yule

Silent Frights: A Collection of Christmas Creepypastas to Chill Your Bones

Santa Raptor's Jolly Carnage: A Dino-Claus Christmas Tale

Prehistoric Palettes: A Dino Wicca Coloring Journey

The Christmas Wishkeeper Chronicles

The Starlight Sleigh: A Holiday Journey

Elf Secrets: The True Magic of the North Pole

Candy Cane Conjurations

Cooking with Kids: Recipes Under 20 Minutes

Doctor Who: The TARDIS Confiscation

The Anxiety First Aid Kit: Quick Tools to Calm Your Mind

Frosty Whispers: A Winter's Tale

The Infinite Key: Unlocking the Secrets to Prosperity, Resilience, and Purpose

The Grasping Void: Why You'll Regret This Purchase

Astrology for Busy Bees: Star Signs Simplified

The Instant Focus Formula: Cut Through the Noise

The Secret Language of Colors: Unlocking the Emotional Codes

Sacred Fossil Chronicles: Blank Journal

The Christmas Cottage Miracle

Feeding Frenzy: Graboid-Inspired Recipes

Manifest in Minutes: The Quick Law of Attraction Guide

The Symbiote Chronicles: Doctor Who's Venomous Journey

Think Tiny, Grow Big: The Minimalist Mindset

The Energy Key: Unlocking Limitless Motivation

New Year, New Magic: Manifesting Your Best Year Yet

Unstoppable You: Mastering Confidence in Minutes

Infinite Energy: The Secret to Never Feeling Drained

Lightning Focus: Mastering the Art of Productivity in a Distracted World

Saturnalia Manifestation Magick: A Guide to Unlocking Abundance During the Solstice

Graboids and Garland: The Ultimate Tremors-Themed Christmas Guide

12 Nights of Holiday Magic

The Power of Pause: 60-Second Mindfulness Practices

The Quick Reset: How to Reclaim Your Life After Burnout

The Shadow Eater: A Tale of Despair and Survival

The Micro-Mastery Method: Transform Your Skills in Just Minutes a Day

Reclaiming Time: How to Live More by Doing Less

Chronovore: The Eternal Nexus

The Mind Reset: Unlocking Your Inner Peace in a Chaotic World

Confidence Code: Building Unshakable Self-Belief

Baby the Vampire Terrier

Baby the Vampire Terrier's Christmas Adventure

Celestial Streams: The Content Creator's Astrology Manual

The Wealth Whisperer: Unlocking Abundance with Everyday Actions

The Energy Equation: Maximize Your Output Without Burning Out

The Happiness Algorithm: Science-Backed Steps to Joyful Living

Stress-Free Success: Achieving Goals Without Anxiety

Mindful Wealth: The New Blueprint for Financial Freedom

The Festive Flavors of New Year: A Culinary Celebration

The Master's Gambit: Keys of Eternal Power

Shadowed Secrets: Groundhog Day Mysteries

Beneath the Burrow: Lessons from the Groundhog

Spring's Whispers: The Groundhog's Prediction

The Limitless Mindset: Unlock Your Untapped Potential

The Focus Funnel: How to Cut Through Chaos and Get Results

Bold Moves: Building Courage to Live on Your Terms

The Daily Shift: Simple Practices for Lasting Transformation

The Quarter-Life Reset: Thriving in Your 20s and 30s

The Art of Shadowplay: Building Your Own Personal Myth

The Eternal Loop: Finding Purpose in Repetition

Burrowing Wisdom: Life Lessons from the Groundhog

Shadow Work: A Groundhog Day Perspective

Love in Bloom: 5-Minute Romantic Gestures

The Shadowspell Codex: Secrets of Forbidden Magick

The Burnout Cure: Finding Balance in a Busy World

The Groundhog Prophecy: Unlocking Seasonal Secrets

Nog Tales: The Spirited History of Eggnog

Six More Weeks: Embracing Seasonal Transitions

The Lumivian Chronicles: Fragments of the Fifth Dimension

The Groundhog's Shadow: A Tale of Seasons
Burrowed Insights: Wisdom from the Groundhog
Sensual Strings: The Art of Erotic Bondage
Whispered Flames: Unlocking the Power of Fire Play
Forgotten Shadows: A Guide to Cryptids Lost to Time
Six Weeks of Secrets: Groundhog Day's Hidden Messages
Shadows and Cycles: Groundhog Day Reflections
The Art of Love Letters: Crafting the Perfect Message
Romantic Getaways at Home: Turning Your Space into Paradise
Purrfect Brews: A Cat Lover's Guide to Coffee and Companionship
The Groundhog's Wisdom: Timeless Lessons for Modern Life
The Shadow Oracle: Groundhog Day as a Predictor
Emerging from the Burrow: A Journey of Renewal
The Language of Love: Learning Your Partner's Love Style
Authorpreneur: The Ultimate Blueprint for Writing, Publishing, and Thriving as an Author
Weathering the Seasons: Groundhog Day Perspectives
Valentine's Day Magic: A Guide to Romantic Rituals
The Shadow Chronicles: Stories of Groundhog Day
Love and Laughter: Fun Games for Valentine's Day
AstroRealty: Unlocking the Stars for Property Success
The Groundhog's Path: A Guide to Seasonal Balance
Groundhog Day Diaries: Reflections in the Shadow
The Groundhog's Light: Illuminating the Path Ahead
Valentine's Traditions from Around the World
AI Wealth Revolution: Unlocking the Trillionaire Mindset
Love Rekindled: Reigniting Passion in Relationships
Single and Thriving: Self-Love on Valentine's Day
Emerald Legends: Mystical Tales of Ireland
Green Alchemy: Harnessing Nature's Magic
The Hearts of Horror: A Valentine's Day Nightmare

The Leprechaun's Guide to Wealth and Wisdom

Dancing with the Sidhe: Celebrating the Otherworld

Shamrocks and Shadows: Mysteries of the Green Isle

Emerald Energy: Harnessing Luck and Growth

The Gingerbread Golem's Valentine: A Sweetheart's Guide to Love and Enchantment

The Celtic Knot: Weaving Life and Destiny

Green Fire: Elemental Magic for St. Patrick's Day

Clover Chronicles: Finding Your Inner Luck

Ireland's Mystical Creatures: A Field Guide

Gingerbread Golem's Love Almanac

Prowl and Thrive: The Lion's Guide to Success

Love Alchemy: Transforming Your Life Through Heart Energy

WORLD DOMINATION: Woman's Rule 3:The New Life

The Midnight Rose: A Guide to Lunar Love Spells

The Forbidden Letters: Writing Your Own Love Prophecy

Luck and Lore: St. Patrick's Day for Modern Mystics

The Green Path: A Pagan Celebration of Renewal

The Dark Architect's Guide to Reprogramming Reality

Prankster's Paradise: A Guide to Harmless Hijinks

Manifest Your Reality: The Law of Attraction Simplified

The TARDIS Owner's Manual: Understanding the Doctor's Ship: *A complete guide to the TARDIS, its technology, secrets, and mysteries*

Starlit Romance: Astrology Secrets for Finding True Love

The Time Lord's Atlas: A Complete Guide to the Whoniverse: *A breakdown of the locations, planets, and dimensions explored in Doctor Who*

Sweetheart Shadows: The Dark Side of Love and Attraction

February Fire: Reigniting Passion in Every Area of Life

The Self-Love Toolkit: 5 Ways to Embrace Who You Are

February Sparks: Ignite Your Dreams in 28 Days

The Magick of Motherhood: Reclaiming Your Power Through Rituals

The Pagan Path to Self-Love: A Goddess's Guide to Worth and Confidence

Wild Woman Magick: Unleashing Your Primal Power

The Money Magnet Blueprint: Unlocking Unlimited Wealth

Biohacking 101: Unlock Your Body's Full Potential

The Wild Father: A Pagan Guide to Strength and Wisdom

The Sacred Masculine: Unlocking Your Inner Power

The Druid's Compass

The Warrior's Mindset

The Father's Fire

Odin's Path

Ancestral Bonds

The House That Whispers

The Magician's Code

The Wild Hunt

The Green Man's Path

The Altar of Success

The Shadow and the Sword

The High Priestess's Guide to Energy Healing

The Lunar Mother

The Sacred Self-Care Grimoire

The Womb Wisdom Codex

The Wheel of the Mother

The Witch's Guide to Manifestation

The Q2 Reset

The Ultimate Guide to AI-Powered Passive Income

Escape the 9-5

AI Feline Fortunes

The Tear-Stained Grimoire

Razorblade Runes

Cemetery Sirens

The Midnight Wristwatch
The Town That Forgets
AI Horror & Creepypasta
The Hollow Frequency
The Breach Echo
The Quiet Between Worlds
The Sigil of Tharan-Khul
Summon the Vault of Y'ha'ten
The Becoming Codex
The Profit of Az'ra-nar
The Drowned Logos
Echoes of the Eldritch Will
The Deep Ledger
Necronomicon of Networth
Covenant of the Wealthwyrm
The Whisperer's Manifesto
The Rites of Azh-K'luth
The Ark of the Crawling Coin
The Tithe of Shadows
Inkheart Abyss
The Timewinds of Y'ha-nthlei
The Spiral Labyrinth of Azag-Nirrh
The Gallifreyan Heresy of the Black Pharaoh
The Psalms of Nyog-Sotha
Black Rain Alchemy
The Infinite Maw
The Entropic Blueprint
The Oracle of Sh'guul
The Book of Breach
The Drowned Saint's Testament
Dreamcraft of the Sleeper God
The Silence Market
Cthonomics: The Dark Wealth Algorithm

Invocation of the Ten-Eyed King
Wealthbound to the Wyrm Below
Become the Unnameable
Codex of the Sovereign Flame
Rituals of Relentless Becoming
The Shadow Ascends
The Eyes Beneath You
The Will That Wakes Worlds
Silence Is a Weapon
The Mirror That Screams
The Whisper Between Moments
The Mind That Devours Fear
The Myth of the Finished Self
The Architect of Your Madness
The Voice You've Buried
The Discipline of Madness
Stormborn: Awakening Your Inner Tempest
The Mind That Ate Time
Unbind Your Becoming
The Pact You Owe Yourself
The Devourer's Diet
The Acid That Carves the Path
The Tower You Must Burn
The Breath Between Worlds
Speak Like the Deep
The Labyrinth Within
The Spine of the Sea God
Rejection Is a Portal
The Crown You Refused
The Scar Is the Spell
The Lightless Flame
The Habit of Becoming Horrific
ChickenJockey Chaos

The Gatekeeper Within

You Are Not Your Name

The Compass of the Mad

The Archive of Unsent Letters

What the Mirror Can't Show You

The Knife You Needed

Worship Nothing, Become Everything

The Other Voice

The Body the World Forgot

The Vein of the Void

The Black Bone Codex

The Puzzle of the Hidden Self (Millennium Puzzle)

The Eye That Sees the Lie *(Millennium Eye)*

The Ring of Return (Millennium Ring)

The Rod of Relentless Will *(Millennium Rod)*

The Tally of the Soul (Millennium Tauk/Necklace)

The Key to the Locked Timeline (Millennium Key)

The Scale of Sacred Decisions (Millennium Scales)

Inferno Bites: The UnOfficial Minecraft Lava Cookbook

Rot in the Attic

Prana: The Hidden Force of Your Infinite Self

The Shadow Realm Within: Transforming Darkness Into Destiny

The Borderland Collapse

Claws of Protection: Bastet's Defensive Magick

Mr. Ring-a-Ding's Madness

Yugioh Astrology: Celestial Deckcraft and Duel Destiny (2026–2027 Edition)

The Seal You Signed: Unlocking the Power You Once Feared

The Puzzle of Infinite Minds: Unlocking the Mentalism Hidden Within

The Eye That Mirrors the All: Secrets of Inner Reflection

Doctor Who: The Toymaker's Broadcast

Rootwake: The Carbon Covenant

Skitter Logic: Unlearning the Fear That Built You

Doctor Who: The World That Froths

Rootwake: The Fizz That Rewrites Flesh

Rootwake: Frothfather of the World

The Holly Pact: Blood Beneath the Mistletoe

The 2nd Mass Principle: Building Unbreakable Tribes

Web of Wits: A Survival Guide to Encounters with Anasi the Spider (Aunt Nancy)

The Hexbreaking Handbook: Effective Spells to Remove Curses

Pop Alchemy: Transform Your Life One Sip at a Time

The Mason Code: Leading in Unleadable Times

Petosiris and the Fifth Chamber of Thoth

The Ether Seed Within

The Parent of Tomorrow

Petosiris's Pyramid of Perpetual Wealth

Unlearn the World

Grimoire of the Hollow Tongue

Zodiac Weeds: Finding Your Strain Through the Stars

Aquarius Rises in the Bank

The Sugar God's Smile

The Skinclock Reversal: Biohacking the Face of Time

Debtburn: How to Obliterate What You Owe Forever

The Ice Cream Oracle: What Your Cone Says About Your Future

Silence Is Sovereignty: The Power of Being Unreadable

The Wind That Whispers Through Stone

Path of the Four Directions

Doctor Who: The Maestro's Symphony of Endings

Oxygen Grail: Breathing to Undo the Clock

Zodiacal Collapse: When Stars Devour Time

Teachings from the Red Sand Silence

Doctor Who: Omega – The Broken Equation
Memory Wipe Your Past: Start Over Like a MiB
Mitochondria Prime: Ignite the Core of Youth
A Nest of Roaches
Grub from the Galaxy: MiB Recipes You'll Never Forget
Whiskers of Power: Bastet's Guide to Inner Sovereignty
The Gift Must Cost Them: Negotiation Through Unequal Exchange

Get Some Tarot cards: https://www.makeplayingcards.com/sell/ apophis-occult-shop

Get some shirts: https://www.bonfire.com/store/apophis-shirt-emporium/

<u>Instagrams:</u>
@apophis_enterprises,
@apophisbookemporium,
@apophisscardshop
Twitter: @apophisenterpr1
 Tiktok:@apophisenterprise
Youtube: @sg1fan23477
Hive: @sg1fan23477
CheeLee: @SG1fan23477

Podcast: Apophis Chat Zone: https://open.spotify.com/show/
5zXbrCLEV2xzCp8ybrfHsk?si=fb4d4fdbdce44dec

Newsletter: https://apophiss-newsletter-27c897.beehiiv.com/

If you want to support me or see posts of other projects that I have come over to: **buymeacoffee.com/mpetchinskg**
I post there daily several times a day

Get your Dinowicca or Christmas themed digital products, especially Santa Raptor songs and other musics. Here:
https://sg1fan23477.gumroad.com

Apophis Yuletide Digital has not only digital Christmas items, but it will have all things with Dinowicca as well as other Digital products.